EMOT

ANGRY

by Genevieve Nilsen

TABLE OF CONTENTS

tadpole
books

ANGRY

He is angry.

3

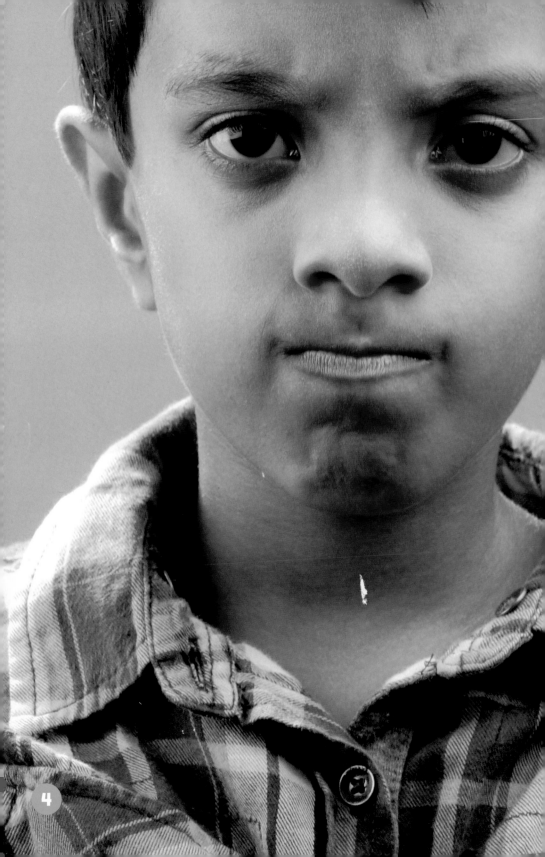

fist

He balls his fist.

She is angry.

She crosses her arms.

He cries.

She yells.

9

She talks about it.

It is okay to feel angry.

He thinks about it.

He feels better.

WORDS TO KNOW

angry

cries

crosses

fist

talks

yells

INDEX